Love & Vodka

Other Books by the Author

POETRY BOOKS
Your Ink on My Soul
In My Own Flood

NOVELS
Crush: A Paranormal Romance Novel
Althia's Awakening
Althia's Calling
Althia's Journey

Love & Vodka

a book of poetry for glass hearts

Christina Strigas

Book design by Maureen Cutajar
www.gopublished.com

CANADA CATALOGUING IN PUBLICATION DATA
Strigas, Christina, 1968-, author
A Book of Poetry for Glass Hearts / poetry by Christina Strigas

ISBN: 978-0-99518653-8

I dedicate this book to . . .

. . . all the people who believe with their hearts.

. . . all the people who keep the rage down until one day it tackled you down.

. . . all the people who believe in the power of words and poetry.

Thank you for being on this journey with me.

Thank you for reading me.

One day in november of 2013 a car crashed into my daycare and I had to save three little girls' lives.

This poetry book is dedicated to the three angels that changed my life and showed me the true meaning of a miracle.

To my children John and Maria:
Never stop dreaming.

Contents

*I loved you for a thousand years
and missed you in all of them*

*I resist you only to wake up
wanting you more inside of me*

Modern love

Talk dirty to me

Tug of war

See you anon

I loved you for a thousand years
and missed you in all of them.

Fragile bird

I could be a fragile bird
a dark raven flying above you
I want to be caged with you
our ankles crossed
staring at the ceiling.

Pleasing

I want to take back words, sentences,
metaphors, idioms and
all the run off sentences you never got. I will
burn them in a pile by
your door. I loved it
when words remained in my desk drawer.
It meant something to know when
and how to use a comma
and periods. They always mattered
to me. It was final somehow.
I knew where you began
and ended. Now everything
is blurred and I type on a tiny screen.
Do you even get it?

If

If the water on the windowsill
could be your molecules
they would give me a paper
to smell
a pen to place safely away
near my utensils
think of me when it rains
how the droplets
become you and me
falling from the sky
like bullets on a battlefield
like trees in the rainforest
sometimes still
most times turbulent
aged and chopped
preserved and honoured.

I am going to think without fear of what you will say let me breathe what air I admire let me paint on an empty canvas instead of burning me under dishes and wash.

I want you mama

All I can say is that the notebooks
are left empty
with their pretty flowers and patterns
inviting me and uninviting me
with the power to fill the pages
of undeniable truths
better left in my thoughts.

All I can think of is how your little hands
were tiny as pebbles are to mountains
and you wished I could not leave you
with a bottle of my nourishment
instead you required my touch
to calm you
and address the pain you are professing
while standing on tables and screaming out
your loss of our seasons together
you say you needed me the most
and kisses blown in the air
and waves by the window
and phone calls left ringing
were never enough
to endure the day.

You asked me about my grandmother
and how she died
your soul was created
as hers was floating away
perhaps you met her along the way
and she passed this resilience
this strong-willed determination
onto your sweet self

to understand that she was just as
confused as you are right now.
Life is simple
children speak the truth
you just want me
and you just need me
so I call you over
and you come lie with me and I tell
you that story about Polly
or Dolly or Pamela or
whatever name pops into my head
and you will look at me with your
big blue eyes and tell me
go on
tell me more
and I go on and on
loving your expressions of pleasure
and imagination. I try to be my best
to you and you try to be your best
to me as your eyes slowly close
to the comfort of my voice.

Ghosts in the hallway

If you turn into an ice cube
I will not melt you with my body heat
but walk through that door and leave it open
a tiny bit
for one footprint.

There's other fish in the sea.

That day and night I did not leave my room or bed.
I cried my soul out.

You'll get over it.

Of course, here I am.

Oh, it was you, who turned into a young man and then
a man and now a middle-aged man full of anxieties.
Perhaps I lack the love to fill your cup up.

He is not the only boy in the world.

And I still think he was the only boy in the world
for me.
My father's voice echoes in me

The pain will get better, you'll see.

And the pain did
and he was right
and now I am trying to unlock my front door
see your shoes in the hallway
but all I see are ghosts
soon I will turn into one too
if you refuse to look at me

I love you.

Conversations with my daughter

-you are not of this world

Why?

-you believe in things that are not real

Like what?

-the universe

It's real. Speak to it. It listens to your thoughts. It's a secret. It holds the keys.

-you see? What are you saying?

One day, you'll understand.

-you're not realistic

No, in this you're right, but it's okay to dream. I've always been this way.

-you're different

For now, just listen to the silence. There are signs everywhere.

-where are they?

Like that cop, who almost gave me a ticket. The Universe is telling me to slow down.

-well, you were driving fast

You see. You're getting closer already. Just look for your signs.

-what are they?

Only you will know them. They're your signs not mine.

Some abandoned tweets

Do you think you are the only one who can revive art?
Do you think art is at your feet or in your heart?
I mostly want to jump onto your back while you
twirl me around and you decide where I land.
At your feet or in your heart, proclaiming
art is not dead, just modern, financed by
social media sites. You know my heart
beats differently when I wear it on
my sleeve, you know my love is
altering like the hatred in
your eyes. Your haunting
look can read me without
words.I break myself in
half only to be reborn
again all in the name
of this fucking art.
These are not il-
Lusions, but dis-
Illusions, bear
with me for no-
thing is ever
done, it just
continues on
into another
poem that I
write for
only you
to read
and to
love.

Open cuts

i don't believe in short
stories
short cuts
fuses. in a long line-up
i read urban slang
for fun. i say thank
you and bless you
and from time to time

fuck you

because
i really want to say

i love you.
but you make it
so hard.

Zeus

It seems we have this neglected approach
to African dresses and lost stitching. she's
so confused with her choice of coffee
that love is not even on the menu
she cried in my car because she
saw those girls having fun,
loving each other, neglecting her.
so fuck the social media, fuck
the "in your face play by play
action of petty lives." she gets it
and is only fourteen, but i sell
it to lovers, dreamers,
i write it mostly for you
but you're gone
into the
mist.
It gets foggy, and rainy,
i wake up to see the sunsets,
nothing changes but my
storage on my phone.
you like my new poem?
you don't even read me. you
prefer to touch me
in my sleep. wake me in my
death. i'm still a vampire, i joke.
you bite my neck and
slap my ass.
you kiss my wounds
and patch up my scars
with silence.
you know i'm giving
everything up soon.

it's written in the palm
of my hand.
the final act.
i take a bow
for the new play.
it's going to be
so dirty
and raw.
this is nothing.
it's tragic how
Greek mythology
was a million years ago,
i'd rather live then
and believe in Zeus
and wait for you
to become a part of me.

Loving a Writer

loving a writer is only for the strong,
the ones who care to stare
at the sky with you. or at a locked door.
you refuse to open. and this is why
love remains crazy. undefined. unbearable.
irrational. because loving a writer
has no rules. it's like seeing the
world for the very first time.

Used Up

say what you have to say
under a mosaic of music
and glitter, old rehashed
words with new meanings
to drive home the hurt
along my west highway.
bring on the hurt, your
warped version of my
cunning ways. but not
with words, rhymes,
streams of consciousness,
none of that bullshit.
you should've played
me like a piano,
not a used up broken-
stringed guitar.

Oceans Away

i still remember that time
when you
caught your breath.
it feels like you're
holding on tight
from oceans away
and lifetimes apart.

The Art in Me

if you could just dare
to fuck the art in me.
the kind of sex
that would put
us both on fire.
the part where you
never leave in
the morning. i
disappoint you
all the time,
with my past,
my present,
my unstable future.
if you could just dare
to love me,
none of it would even matter.

Untitled

did you know

your absence makes me forget my presence?

i never got your attention
when I needed it the most.

i want to tell myself
to shut the fuck up. to
not think of the silence
between us. my mind is
on the moon. on its
constant daily impact.
not just the new moon
or the blood moon.
but The Moon. i tell
myself to relive the
moments we placed our
feet in the water. the
way we danced together.
it's on camera. and
i watch us and cry.
creating notes to myself
in battle with each other.

nothing hurts me more
than myself. my doubts
my prescriptions,
my doses of you.
you make me hit
brick walls, smash my knees
against your back, no

troubles are dug up, i create
them, paint them like Renoir,
describe them like Marquez.
can't you see my magic
realism? thought you'd
see through it all.
but, alas
you blinded me
and yourself
again.

another day of missing you
of wanting you
to do all those things
you wrote about.
another day of typing
with no ribbon.
of thinking of you
in empty dreams.
another hollow day.

Brooklyn

i hope you realize
that covers will not
keep you away. words
will steal the night
from us. music will
drain the veins.
my undergarments
will vanish. trickery
in the city.
do you see
me
on the street
with Brooklyn
in my eyes
and water
around us?
i float and swim

while you take the bus
to Chinatown.

*I resist you only to wake up
wanting you more inside of me.*

Waking up to I love you.
Only from your voice.
It is the one that changes
my dark to light. Brings
out my love of beauty
and the love
you saw in me.
I want to wake up
to those three
words. Feel them
upon my skin.

You know
what to not say.
This is the reason.

- *I am yours.*

it's not the way
you leave
it's the way
you come back
it's how you
remember
when i forget.

- *it's how you are*

what i miss most
about you
is everything
we didn't do
and everything
we said
we would.

- *a tweet*

Death changes
the current
in your heart.
when it suddenly hits you
makes your heart ache
how you will never see
his face again. Ever.

- *my dad*

i'm not sure about you
but what if we were to
pretend that from here
on in,
the past
does not matter
as much as you think.
pretend the future
is the fresh cup
of coffee,
and the present
the cigarette in
your mouth.
just light it.

- *carpe diem*

i think the way the sun shines on you
has nothing to do with the sun
but everything
to do with you.

- *your magic*

if poetry
music
books
art
sky
ocean
don't make you cry
you should stare longer
read more
listen with your soul.

- *i want to write you into everything i do*

all the parts of me
i did not show you
were the ones
i wanted you
to notice.

- *perception*

the longer the silence remains
untouched
the longer the miscommunication
creates its own stories.

- *soul communication*

tear me apart
rip me into pieces
throw me to the wind
and bury me
with poems
no earth
no flowers
just words
in death
cover me
with notes.

*- when i feel too much and the universe
aches inside of me*

you sense my storm and lock down your windows
tight
but i am already inside.

- *you carry me*

the only way to find art
is to lose touch
with reality.

- pour some art on me

you can't break up with a soul mate.

- *true story*

I'm an open book
in a closed room.

- *read me*

when I was in your hands
you let me slip
away. my words were
oil and yours were
water. it was volcanic
the ashes
were left. it was
your hands that led
me to your car. we
made the back seat
sink with jealousy.
i fell from the sky
in 1987 and your hands
held me tight.

- back seat poetry

i could not tell you
for
you did not want
to hear.
you pretend to be
tough. no matter
how smart you are,
or how many times
your words sting
my soul,
i remain
still.

- *like water*

hard to love you
when you put up
concrete fences.
be gentle.
your anger
builds more
sand dunes
to my deluge.

- *how deep is your water*

what i miss most
are all the things
we never did.

- *reality*

I see the beauty in you and the darkness.
Both are brilliant.

-third eye

Modern love

Embracing the pain

you can switch your
judgments over to the
side of the road, park
your car in the middle
of a traffic jam to
text me you love me.
i'm embracing the pain,
hating the crime that
got me here in the
first place. and i
have no idea where
the fuck you are,
or who you're chasing now,
or why you forgot
everything I ever told you.

but, darling, i remember everything.

Window

Open up the window
let it out
get down on my scraped
ten year old knees
do nothing but shout
about how
epiphanies come alive
how we bend our minds
to strive
for these words that haunt
memories that jaunt
to remind me of how
it used to be
in my mother's arms
in my father's embrace
that comfort I need to face
to feel again
in an imagined place
at this time when
you make a question
into life lessons
as if a gate has opened
once locked
a dam blocked
and you
the boat
slipping endlessly by
as I wait afloat.
When you hear my voice
swearing about the knots
it has a complete familiarity in itself

talking to myself, all alone
laying my soul on its shelf.
How modern love has come to this
words and voices we miss
modern sex without a kiss
evolved to pictures
erotica unsolved
mysterious you
hilarious me
exchanging thoughts on a leafless tree
as Fall echoes the emptiness
we lay it out bare and confess
to nothing we did not
know before
yet all we want is more
of this and that
skinny and fat lattes in the Montreal cold
to warm the bones
let the truth unfold.
The windows are shut tight
to not let in the air
it chills my bare body
lets down my messy hair
and somehow you are in the room
no longer locked out
as I sweep with my broom
all the dark sorrow that I want
to live without
you hold on to my run
and ask me
are you ready to chase the sun?

The Bridge Interlude

The closer I come
the further you feel.
I could not tell you
for you did not want to know
then I did not want the truth
no matter its profound beauty
it is hard to look at your shadow
for so many months
hard to love you
when you put up concrete fences.
On that full moon
I would tell nobody
die with it
live with it
breathe with it
why ask at all?
I wore my high heeled blue shoes.
Someone may know more than you
and so ready to peek inside my soul
while you sleep awake
and wonder about fate.
I am starting to not trust the internet
and it all started in Soho
the information lied
your hopefulness
my mood swings
my answers
your neighbourhood.
Little things tell me what you want
and it may not be

so deep inside of me
as I first thought
it could be as far away as oceans are
safe from my loneliness.
Relying on technology and shoes to get me places
closer to you
when in essence
it is further away.

Naked

Naked before you with my tight jeans
snug top
cleavage
blue high heeled sandals
words between us like sand
in an ocean
and you say I make you crazy
while I breakdown
have my mid-life crisis too late
waiting for sundown
to run into the night
naked
embrace the demons
talk to them
comfort them
control and lose control of them
while you watch my bra strap
come undone
and you stay so close
you never run
to my other side
but you want my bedside
my naked soul
to devour
not just the skin
the game of lose or win
is long gone
play the same song
to feel my heartbeat
my retreat
into you and your essence.

Melodic Voices

Cold days of thunder
summer songs with 80's beat
violin, chants
on my back, side, stomach
sleepless,
even a cake in the middle of night
will not revive the memories
bones ache, heart resonates
melodic voices sing their truth
come with a pack of smokes
and lies
I will be waiting
listening to the three a.m. sounds
comforting, hurting,
blades of grass
skin to skin
full moon
and still we are tied
to invisible ropes.

Toast

By the time the toast pops
I have created a few lines of
a story in my head that includes a character
with your nickname. Wouldn't you like
that? You always wanted to be in
my stories, but deep down
I think you don't. You just want to
pretend that you do so I could love you more
or less. I have to spread the butter now.
Toast popped and hands are sticky.

a crash inspired

Varicose veins are extending
they have a life of their own –
the moon Diana is blending
with our concept of time we have always known
while fragments of our lives are deceiving
the distinct plots we are weaving.
Act one is coming to an end
and the letter I never wrote nor will ever send
is altering every instant we are apart.
Oh, how sweet it would be to return to the start
the line that fades with acid rain
the lines on my forehead receding in pain.

You talk the talk but never show me
the action you decree
let me not look into your hypnotic eyes
one more time. I'll try to rise
up out of this trance you mix
hold out your hand to mine to fix
the cracks on the sidewalk
the mangled thoughts I so want to talk
for only your ears to listen
and my heart to break or win
this agonizing race of spirits
that follow me to my wits
and stop before the end approaches
as if to say that love is dead,
yet afire with yellow-flamed torches
leading to the path of uncertainty.
Along my neck your curious fingers
travel to uncover me,

continue discovering all my entrances
and omit my exit from my rhymed sentences
remember, the skin will never stop this change,
we walk the same road in every age,
so maybe you would like to join me in this futile,
self-absorbed love
or perhaps you would much rather observe
the innocent whiteness of the dove?
I know I missed the sense of trust
you sang about with an abundance of lust
but believe me I see everything -
I especially adore it when you sing
of a moment that never was between us,
I promise I will not make a fuss
about the texture of the grass
or the unique shape of your ass
just keep on walking down that path
I'll see you in grade 9 math
and we will start another book
of cities we never traveled and one unused hook
that marks our name with a hyphen
signed papers at an old Southern church way back
when
we died at that car crash
our heads through the dash
and into the golden satin curtain
of this love so thick, yet thin.

The wind is the sign that hope is alive

She was in love with an ideal
way before he came into her life and ate her whole
he wanted to cut her up and save a piece everyday
but she refused the sharp touch of his blade
she fell deep into a well
and no one heard her CRIES
except the
W I N D
that never showed her the way out
years she suffered in anguish
(while he came and went as he pleased taking
everything with him as he slept and ate under the
same roof)
till finally she saw the
S I G N
it was a dull August morning
no clouds in the Montreal sky (for once)
and he came home early with a book
just for her
*some writer was selling her books at the corner of Peel
and Ste. Catherine. Can you believe it?*
she took the book like a drug addict takes his fix
and read it in one day
she did not get out of bed
it was an awful book
filled with spelling mistakes
and run-on sentences

but
also full of
H O P E
she knew she could do it
she bought
some journals from Dollarama
with black lines and purple lines
and wrote a story
he watched her
and he went out and bought her more books
he went to book launches and met writers
and finally he saw her
A L I V E
and he read every word she wrote.

Watching Anna Karenina

When that empty breeze
brings upon memories
of how your kisses tasted so sweet
your arms around my neck
gently lifting me
the white love surrounding
us on the green grass
and how I bit your lip
in ecstasy
and teased you
until the fights turned
into mad sex
meeting lovers in corridors
behind screens
and how love stands alone
blocks cages and church icons
as anger is the new breed
of communication
while you look down my blouse
hard for me
wanting all of me my insides filled with only you
if I could give you more of me
I would
but I am stuck
somewhere between who I was
and who I want to be
for I am on that unpredictable wave
forecast is fluctuating
my insides are tortured
with common folk

but your eyes
oh those fucking eyes
how they see through every piece
of me
that I toss and shed off
like my clothes
naked.
You can undress me
without a touch
love me
until we speak no more
of this
or silence me
with no words
that make me search for my own.
It is how you pursue me
without wanting to
battling yourself
me
Us
Them
Him
Her.
It is the death of us that preoccupies my mind
rather than the birth.
One can die from a broken heart
and princesses and princes
are not immune
to clutching their heart
in torment.

No one can truly
forgive betrayal.
I watch your strong back
as I leave you
no other choice
but to say goodbye
to the woman you
kissed on that fall day
and who loved you
with all her breath.

Tell me

tell me about the magic
tickling the back of your throat.

tell me why you forgot
your wallet when you saw me.

tell me why you didn't
break down all my walls.

tell me why you stopped asking questions.

tell me if you forgot my curves.

tell me you'll still
drive fast
to get to me.

tell me why I'm
wrong about you.

tell me why you and i
still exist.

tell me the reason
you lied.

tell me why you feel
names are not important.

tell me why you left me
when you
wanted to meet me.

tell me why you never
loved me from across
a room.

tell me whatever is on
your mind,
i'm listening.

Talk dirty to me

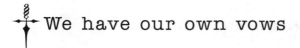 # We have our own vows

when I was reckless, you drove my car.
when I was doubtful, you read my book.
when I was needy, your arms felt safe.
when I was mournful, you wiped my tears.
when I ran, you caught up to me.
when I drank, you held back my hair.
when I lost the baby, you cried with me.
when I gave birth, you were my rock.
when I slept on the couch, you slept there with me.
when I met you at sixteen,
we met again every year after that.
when we fight, me make up.
when we make up, we remember
why we have
the same ring.
when you fuck me,
we still make love.
when you meet a soul mate
you never break up.

Conversations of matter

Do you want to fuck me?
Always, when you ask like that.
Like what?
So honestly.
Do I make you wet?
Yes.
That one word makes me hard.
Now it's my turn.
Go ahead, baby.
Do you want to fuck me?
Oh, so very much.
Do I make you hard?
The hardest I've been.
Can it be destroyed?
Never.
Can we create?
Always. Now bring that sexy
ass over here and let me show
you what these hands
can do to that body to replace
these words.

Working Hard

He said he thought of me every morning and I
made him hard.
He touched himself in the middle of the day. He
couldn't work.
He wanted me so badly.

Just knowing how he felt, made me so wet, all I
thought about
was what he said.

I wanted him to keep on telling me how I affected
him, but one day he stopped. He went away across
Canada; disappearing off the face of life.

From time to time, I remember him. He had changed
his name so many times, I no longer knew which was
the right one, which was the wrong one. I knew who
he really was and I will keep this secret along with
all the other ones he told me deep in a secret locket
of my soul.

Everything he said to me still makes me smile.
Then I cry. Then I drink.

Sex drops

You dropped yourself
inside of me,
as I squeezed my legs
to keep you there.
I watched every drop
eat me up. Absorb me.
Define me.
I wanted to eat you alive.
I opened my mouth
and swallowed you whole.
How you moaned. Groaned.
Pulled my hair
and
turned me over
told me to keep quiet.
Touched my neck,
slapped my ass,
and
fucked me
with my t-shirt still on.

The Wedding Reception

Yes, I'm on fire. Yes, my clitoris is calling your
name.
Yes, I want to cum and feel you so deep inside of
me.
Yes, I want to make you hard
from across the room,
from across the table,
in front of this crowd.

"Meet me in the bathroom," I write on a tiny napkin
and accidentally drop it in your lap.

Your cock is so hard, I gasp. When I slide my pant-
ies to the side, no sooner do I feel your thrust enter
my fucking soul.

I've known you for ten years,
but never like this.
You fuck me silently
covering my mouth,
whispering dirty words
in my ear so only I could hear.
The movement between us is art.
I realize this is the fuck
I have waited for my whole life.

What makes it perfect is my wedding dress is so
tight, you can't touch my nipples, and this makes
me so hot,
as your body moves
the sweet scent of the red rose,
matching my bouquet,
emits a love
only a bride and groom
could smell.

Sext

Send me a picture of you right now.

I'm in a meeting.

Go to the fucking bathroom.

Hold on.

So I send him one,
I'm wearing a cheetah print thong
the one he loves.

You're so hot, I can't concentrate.

But I've heard it so often, how my beauty distracts
him. He wants me to be his dirty little whore at
noon.

So I touch myself in the bathroom
like he wants me to.
How he aches for me, he says, he can't take it.

Is this going in your fucking book? he asks.

Nothing is real, I reply.

Awakenings

something naughty
something nice
I'm a balance
on your sexual tightrope.

even if you don't believe me.

you have awakened
the locked up parts,
the ones that melt
at your look,
as my clothes
fall on the floor,
your hands
on my hips,
your whispers
on my lips,
as we become
midnight
seductions.

draw some blood from my lips
as you bite
a little too hard,
and I like it.

it's not what you do wrong
It's what you do right
and all these moments
haunt me
wake me up
from life
like your eyes
looking down on me
from under you,
as my naked body
fires up
for your engine.

Nothing is a coincidence

You made me into someone
you wanted
to fuck,
and I loved
my
transformation.

You made me love you,
you, and your sexy wit,
ready with a comment,
an update on humanity,
a song for the broken hearted,
a song for the sunsets,
sunrises.

My city is not the same
without you. I still
drive down St-Denis
street, the tragedy
of your ghost's kiss
gone,
from this lifetime.

I reached poetic zones
with you,
you were like a shot of vodka,
truth serum for the soul.

I may be a romantic,
but
know that I am
never hopeless.

Did you feel the brilliance? you asked,
the hues of the sky need you, you said.
Whisper your secrets to the wind,
Listen to the messages in the stars.

It was a conversation that
poets understood.
Lovers confirmed,
naysayers denied.
It was the meanings behind
the lyrics.

Love or lust

first it's my eyes
then it's your heart
pounding. Your kiss
lights my soul. My
love for you empties
the darkness. what's
left of us? you ask.

the lust. the desire.

your arms around me,
drowning my river
turning me slowly
into all you crave.

love and lust me.

my body and soul
and mind
are waiting.

as are my legs
ready to wrap them
around your waist.

Love and Vodka

it was the vodka
combined with your eyes
that gave me your
love in a shot glass.
i drank all of you
and wanted more.
the vodka killed me
the cigarettes destroyed me,
but your love
it fucking created me.

Deep kisses

kisses on the cheek
neck
earlobe
shoulder
waist
hips
languorous
ravenous kisses
in all the places
i didn't mention
the spots you are thinking
about right now
take my breath away
with your kiss
your touch.

those deep kisses
the ones Leonard Cohen
laments. please. more
than a thousand of them.
so many more.

Tug of war

Tug-of-war

When you enter the hallway
search for your shoes
I see the curve of your back
and I remember
the horse you rode on
years ago
in another act
where cars were wider
where cassette decks overpowered
the streets.

The door is wide open
you know I hate
to look at a dirty toilet bowl
or a hair filled sink;
the car outside is not starting
and today is a holiday again.
I have to stay home
cook with love
leave the written papers
in my drawer filled with socks
notes
long forgotten about existed.
Your voice is slowly
settling as it fades away
I ignore it as I run the water
Loud
so I can clean that stain.
For how long do I have to scrub
to erase you from my mind –
I guess, forever.

You are not going anywhere
you want to make coffee
and you insist I make it so
much better.

Have I ever told you
I love it when you bend
to pick up a piece of dirt
from the floor?
or when you rub
my bad shoulder
or care about the laundry?
But the phone rings
and you have tugged the rope
so hard
I am falling on the Mexican tile
not wanting to pull my side
my bad arm hurts
so I let go.

The Appointment

Waiting for the doctor
to see my insides
smell of curry in the waiting room
foreign languages surround me
like a mob
  saris
    beads
      black eyeliner

green and white striped socks
don't match and don't intend to
  babies
    toddlers
      pregnancies
I am only checking my uterus
  for any sign of death
paying for Pap smears
  without blinking an eyelash.

Empty toilet paper rolls
  peeing standing up
hurting my pelvis.

Pashminis of every color
  mine is a lilac
reminds me of our trip to Italy.
Bright shades envelop me
in every mixed color imaginable
as long as they are warm

who cares about
the boots
  with holes
    and worn-out socks
at least we are not barefoot
being hit by cars
  living in tents
    drinking deplorable water
      and calling out Master.

I have the eye of the tiger
in my deep jean pocket.

She smiles at me
as I hold the door open
dark, hurtful eyes
wondering if I'm the enemy too.

I love the silver threaded beads
so closely aligned.

Did she sew them
  or her mother
    no longer with her
left behind in a war zone
  of shredded limbs
    and crumbled homes.

I am waiting on the same doctor
who lives in the city
that has altered
yet hasn't.
She has more gray hairs
a few extra pounds,
says she's leaving Quebec
(second one in five years).

A pinch of every spice
is waiting to be boiled.
Montreal is ever-changing.

Decades ago
others thought the same way
about my flesh and blood
now under the cold brown terrain.

I cross the street
  after the appointment
and my open-stretched legs
baring all
and the child-bearing years
slowly dissipating
as I approach the chapter
of the mammogram.
Phew, I'm still too young, she said.

So I walk into my shiny new car
throw some thoughts under my tires
like how
  I didn't want to hang up my coat
like how
  I searched for a chair close to the window
like how
  I didn't understand a spoken word
like how
I looked out on Victoria and Van Horne street
to find some comfort
and there it was: Second Cup.

The nurse said, I look good for 40.

Now, I am waiting for an examining room
to see what no one can see.
I listen to broken French
end-of-day chatter,
cell phone on silent.
I am frozen in the corridor
next to
a little girl with tight braids
and a crooked part.
After that dreaded ordeal
and awkward questions

I park my car in my driveway
in the suburbs
and I ponder
how a caterpillar
can turn into a butterfly
and why is
the reverse never possible.

This Anger

Angry words remain alive
for years
after they have been spoken
they can never be returned
once said
they start to ferment
grow into another type of plant
you never read about before
and your garden roots begin to transform
into barren wasteland
thirsty earth, left neglected.

Years turn this plump skin
into cracks
and palm readings become necessary
to grasp the future
slowly treading into the boxes of photo albums
left for the children to discover
on their own
upon the death of a loved one.
Show me your anger and wake me up
from this
endless tornado of everyday life.

The Magic

When I see you walk I want
to never leave your motion
and your presence.
You possess that quality in me
that I can never hold
onto for longer than a moment
or a thought in my head now here
now gone.
Standing near you is making me dizzy
with headaches no aspirins
can help
bottles of them are on my nightstand
and I am so tempted to take them all
to escape this spinning of my love
which you walk all over.
Pink shoes in my closet never worn
but a cute little four year old is
enjoying them more than I ever would.
Her sweet kiss is pressed up against my cheek
as my pen continues this line
I am waiting for something magical
to happen
when all the while the magic is in front
of me, talking to me
asking me questions, wanting to know my
words, my grocery lists,
milk, sugar, and love in a bottle.

Contradictions

Observe and contemplate my life
before your affirming eyes
as they emphasize my strong-minded
determination
to persuade you to kiss me
under the mountainous skies
that transform like the weather
into unpredictable situations.

Every romantic lyric is breathing into me
devouring my verve
and my command of the language
is slowly disintegrating into the music.

The opaque light you reflect my way
is mysterious
full of devilish intent
the big bad wolf
is wooing me into this reckless path
of scandal and provocation
instead please read my midnight thoughts
of revelations.
The magic word is discovery
unravel me
interpret my words
detect the scent of no perfume on me
spot the insecurities
and help me overcome
the tragedies of misjudged decisions.
Resolve the disbelief in us
stand next to me even when
I wish you would not.

Blue

Distance grows
months become seconds gone by
I see you so rarely now
I forget your likes
and dislikes
or at least I pretend I do
till sanity slaps me
reminds me of your play on words
and
your allure.

Lines of Insanity

Days pass so quickly
morning turns into night
at the snap of my fingers
you are so far away
yet I hear your words inside me
echoing the silence.
You are talking to me now
and I answer back.
Our conversation is exhilarating
I cannot wait until our next
Encounter.
What are your days filled with?
We are so busy
living our lives
and not truly living them
for without you it seems
so trivial, dutiful.

I wake up at the sound of the alarm
another warm cup of coffee
Columbian
another lonely ride
universal.
You work, you play
you dial to nothingness.
Or perhaps you look at my picture
Somewhere in the back of your desk drawer
Pretending it is not there
and dream of knowing me closer
than this.

Our truth is haunting my restless sleep
it is 3:52 a.m
now it is 4:37 a.m
I close my eyes
cannot break loose from your hold
it is still dawn
so I take a shower
give up on liberating myself
from you.
I imagine your restful sleep
so permanent
while I toss and turn
at sunrises.
Every night is like a road trip
faraway
each kilometer endless
until your destination.

The truth will only tie
me down
never face it
as I would a red light.
Hide my lines of insanity
to honest eyes that love me.
The answers are never spoken
they lie trapped
in a high mountain cave
where slaves worked and died
where you and I
will never run to

we may never kiss or embrace
or play hide-n-seek games
even if we must create stories
to share a moment
of oneness, of connection
it is not pleasurable.
Deceit of oneself
is worse than suicide
for we feel the betrayal
every morning, every second.

Once I was sure
I saw you staring
up at my window
but upon a closer look
it was my imagination
the car was empty
just like my nights
and Romeo and Juliet
was playing again
on Masterpiece Theatre.

I go to see you every
fucking day.
I listen to your favorite
song along the way.
Right above your name
on the cold stone marble cross
I sing you a verse

and the wind streaks my tears.
I miss your voice,
as I try to understand
the day
you never opened your eyes again.

I ask myself
why must I run into you
everywhere I am
when you no longer walk beside me.

I never heard

All these rhymes I never heard
as a teenager come crashing in on me
and persuade me to change the lock
on all my doors
to not let you in
to my thoughts and dreams
but you seem to be deaf to my telepathic
communication as this assumption
of you and I in scrap yards
looking for the missing pieces
as dreadful sharp metal edges
try to cut into our skin
and this heroine must walk so cautiously
on the wrong side.

All these songs I never heard
as an adult come pouring in on me
and remind me of the wrong buttons pushed
on all my body parts
to not allow the pain in
to my intelligence and nightmares
but you are there at the sound of a ring
ready to repair all the delicate misconduct
as liberating words escape my lips
and try to enslave your skin
as this heroine must talk so loudly
on the pretentious side.

Knockdown

i lost all the words with all the thoughts
of you and i in endless meetings
of our minds
let me place them in an envelope
and mail them to you
or maybe not.
i will start over
pretend they are lost in space
for no eyes to read
not yours
not mine.
i remember how i sat up endless
night and days pondering every word
every rhyme
and now you will never read them
i thought i would show them to you
but fate has decided against it.

you were watching me under these lenses
at the wedding we were leaning against the white
fences
i try to imagine you single and available
as i try to recreate this fable:

you walked into the room and you showed me
something that seemed important; a recipe, an
article, i was not really listening to your words,
i just wanted to see your t-shirt
i guess you just wanted to catch a glimpse
of my jeans i wore that day
or smell my lingering perfume in the air

as you spoke i stared at your lips
you did the same
without anyone noticing our eyes.
I sprained my neck watching you drive off,
as the sun beamed in my eyes.
i scream inside
but you cannot hear my voice
or be beside me
for i want to abstain from this adolescent manu-
script
however we march along
this parade of submission
to a higher level.

my lamplight is on while you are at large
my lavender oil is burning
laundry piled up
and i detest the reality shows.
i go rent the saddest love story
and cry myself to sleep
to exonerate your solid existence
that is secretively consuming me.

i want to pester you with so many questions
i want to ask you about the separate lives
we lead and leave
every day as we start the car
up until we cover ourselves with sheets.
the sea remains untouchable
never to jump into it naked
with no free thoughts

our unconscious flowing like the river
our touch drowning the undeniable journey.
this outline is for another knight and princess
to knockdown the barrier between the looking-glass.

let me go now and prepare the day
i do not want to stagnate and struggle
out of this abyss
i want to use you and tolerate all your
daily habits
the hair in the sink won't bother me
as mine mixes with yours
we will let the utmost dirt accumulate
and let it voyage together down the drain
into the river
across the ocean.
it is a whimsical legend I am recounting
just for your eyes, ear, lips, tongue
and you better kiss me now
before i start my car and you never hear this
rich language before you
you better reach over now
before the grass grows and is covered with snow
before the leaves turn maple and walnut
before i open the door
for this moment is only here once
navigating in your direction
understand it
believe it.

i feel nauseous now. you are noble, loyal
let us forget this novella.

See you anon

Messed up

you mess up my head with poems
fuck up my life with songs
read my thoughts before
i grasp them. squeeze them
into verses. wet my skin
with some type of glory
from within. i think i have
lost the way to the rotary,
that fork in the road i
evade, that street that
blocks me from driving.
he kisses me in the dark,
turns on the lights
to see the shimmer
of my skin. he is in love
again, with every
part of my soul that glistens.
he exits and enters
like a king. i danced
just for him, twirled
curtsied and sang
just for him. and he
said he loved
my voice, when that
wasn't what i wanted
him to notice at all.
he's distracted with
soul mates. i'm exploding
on paper.
locked the door

and set my
soul on fire
with words.
no one here gets out alive, i joked.
screaming from my bed,
you're fucking crazy.
pour me some vodka-
my son laughed
and hasn't let go of Jim's book
ever since I brought it home.
I'm trying to write a poetry book
that will make you cry
at least once.
I shout.
but everyone is locked in
their own room
and my coffee cup
is out of vodka.

Muddy Boots

The damp earth moulded you,
two souls side by side like produce
in an aisle,
roasting Easter lamb above our heads.
There they are, she says.
It is when the coffin settles, the sculpted wood
evaporates,
the mud dries on our boots,
the alarm clock rings,
then life grabs you.
Shakes you.
Nothing stands still but the tulips
on my table. Days and hours
mingle like strangers at a party,
a place you get lost in. Moments
when nothing is relevant anymore.
It hits you again, slaps you, whispers in your ear:
*you'll never laugh again the same way as you
did with him*
the joke seems stale now. Dry on your lips.
heavy on your heart. But you say it
you continue to say it. Believe in it.
No crowd roaring as the list
of the dead keeps growing
like our needs.
Still how your beauty wakes me
turns my pain into poetry
my Good Friday into symmetry.

I will always write
do not worry your beautiful mind
about me. I am as you say
messed up,
drinking Metaxa with too much glee
creating words you will never see.
just another poem about death
hashtag death, make it concrete,
or damp like the earth
or kill the spirit
with the typewriter
but oh, how the clicking sound
lifts my soul
closer to yours.
I wiped my boots
clean again,
ready to write poems.

Eating Words

rip me apart into tiny pieces
\ \
put me back together
am I not your human puzzle?
obscure \ \ imagine my skin
concrete\ \ touch my skin
or did you bury me
left me to die
when I told you to do so.
\ \
you know how to put me underground
I spit out dirt
my hands unbound
addicted to you
like all the drugs hidden in cement
while I read all the poets
published or unpublished
poets or so-called poets
self-fulfilled prophecies
running from themselves
\ \
I took poetry like accountants
study numbers
it is an art
to love words
and soak in them
feel them on your tongue
and along the chambers of your heart
it is the soul
\ \

that reads
\\
it came to this
so I could come to you
with words cracked on my lips
syllables forgotten in steamed pots
\\
arrive at my window with tiny pebbles
tap tap tap
in this mad world
into my long forgotten poems
requiring your eyes
to give them life
\\
I tried to let you go
but Muse is telling
me it's madness
and swallowing me whole
\\
breathing and eating words
to write you a love poem
if this could be called that
not so sure
anymore
of what a love poem
is
\\

or why I am using symbols
to show you my love
and how I think of you
every time you don't.
\\
I can go on like this forever
loving you
writing for you.
Long after you have forgotten
all about me.

Drink Nectar

When all else fails, flip my hair and pack on the
make up
fill up the lines with lies
hook up the bra with magnetic propaganda
but Jim keeps whispering to me from the dead
he made me type his every poem
while getting 100
back when typing had a rhythm
back when poets were rare.
Too much crap and bullshit snow
in beginning of spring
yet all the thieves of my heart
are running in the forest
barely visible to humanity
whose heads are bent
with neck spasms.
I studied it alright and took a break
no one is the best and no one is my favorite
a few appointments missed
will not change my life.
I miss you like a writer misses reading
but when I get my fix of modern love
I have to go back to ancient gods
and drink nectar.
I apologize for my messy hair
getting in the way
of your day.
I'll step back
take off my robe
and take pictures
you won't want to see.

Weeds

It must have been three or four in the morning
jumping from one naked bed to the next
imagining weeds growing out of my broken wing
and how some people leave them in the cracks
while others pull and trim.
Every soul needs a rim
every love a first and a last hymn
I don't want to rhyme today
but the other half is in your sunny ray.
Someone pulled me out of my dream
he was tall
and spoke eloquently
with words of a poet
was it you?
Did you feel my naked skin?
The weeds are under the snow now
still -10 in the wind
as well as my heart.
Lying down in examining rooms
being spread out and memorizing
centimetres and numbers
cyst sizes and wild frontiers.
I imagine I would be pretty as a blonde
but I'm okay.
He looked so worried
talking to my old high school teacher
in a waiting room of women

with pretty robes and panoramic views of the city
from the tenth floor.
I'm okay.
I feel like a weed though
I feel stuck between the cracks
and I'm not so sure
if I'm okay at all.

In the Waiting Room

Forgot my notebooks
my appointments locked me up
out of your box for a day
breathed perfectly
shaking off security guards
flirting in front of my daughter
walking in malls
of the living dead.
Watching you charm
the nurses
is he always like this? They ask.
My smiles are tired
my love superb
like a classical piece
Chopin opus 9
its ups its downs
its climax.
I needed that breakdown
to stop me from smoking
drinking
now I feel too much
numb it
with your body on mine
I don't need modern love
too old-fashioned
too old to keep up
I'm so fine
in the waiting room.

My time to write
to heal
among these expert doctors
touching my breasts
my heart
when it belongs to you.
Crying to songs
my vampire make up
smudging my creases.
I am feisty
only he can handle me
in your wildest dreams
you wouldn't want a wife
like me
not even a lover for a day
I'm not that type
not a true artist at all
keeping the drugs
under the pillow
the cancer behind
the counter
where no one can reach.

See you anon

Writing a novel is such a task
words found somewhere on the bottom of a tin flask
one last drop to tie me over
give me luck with a fake four leaf clover.
The dead trees still live
on the icy snow
we pass the farms, the homes
trying to let the feelings go
but they knock
they hum
like the sounds of this train or a long lost battle
drum
on a bumpy ride or a field of dead
drink coffee and hide
behind Gatsby's bed
or samples of another book
about people I never knew
or ones that I want to meet
so I write
on this train
on my feet
on a chair
in my head
up the musical stairs
as long as I paid the fare.
Did you miss my words?
all these crying kids
buy sour cream and onion chips
and then the mirror on the taxi reminds
me of him

fills my head up with deceitful lights
take words and turn them into
the vast forest
spanning across our two provinces
flowing in and out of them as robbers do
trickery, lies and subterfuge
filled with sweet apple pies.
Show my boarding pass
I have 87% of Fitzgerald
can't stop reading about Daisy
Tom and Jay
leave nothing behind
night has turned into day
your name on my lips
and hands tightly squeeze my hips
for the trees are whispering again
and I know
people like us
can only hear them
even from behind the glass.
I write the title first
it's from the book
another route
and cable lines
keep us joined
stronger than poetry.
Grab my bags
I'm coming home
and I missed you too.

Deep penetrating love

I don't care who can see
who is blind to the truth
who sees the truth behind the lies
who reads my poems
who skims through them
like a magazine article.
I don't care who loves art
or museums
as long as you
and I
are in a deep penetrating love
on our knees together
equal
unequal
steady
unsteady
alive
dead
just some pounding love drunk poetry
tipsy on your mid-day words
late night fucks
early morning pick me ups
drag your ass
over here
and kill me to death
under your poetic umbrella
while I lay here
waiting
on the same channel
change my road
lead me to your address
we're all fucking psychos here.

Emergency in Two Parts

1.
If regular days exist
I want to have one
without trauma rooms
injections, life threatening
false alarms and real tragedies.
Spend a day in hallways
rooms which monitor
heartbeats
instead give science lessons
about the four chambers of the heart
(the heart, the body, the soul, the mind)
you just made that up, Mama
I suppose I did.
It is the nasty smell of sickness
versus Gucci floral scents
Diesel *pour homme*
how we fight the system
sign away organs
cry under smiles.
At least the walls are a warm beige
and the *no service* on my phone
gives me time
to reminisce
as my mom and aunt describe
myself at four, five, nine, sixteen
I did that?
How other people's memories
of you
are not even your own
how family

is stuck together
in hospital waiting rooms
taking turns to eat
or smoke or think.
This is how your childhood
smacks you
with scenes
from a forgotten movie
you vaguely recall.
You made Greek coffee at nine
(wow, such an accomplishment)
as their definition of a woman
and mine clash once again.
Yet times means nothing
and memories
are a dream now
what was real, invented,
told to you
what you are doing
in a hospital for twelve hours
when there is absolutely nothing
medically wrong with you
so I write some poems
about moments
slipping away.

2.
Working at a hospital at sixteen
does open up your heart
toughen your soul

evolve your mind
wear out your body
and all that smoking
in staircases discussing the importance
of art
theories
writers
seemed like Nelly and I
would change the world
with our artsy degrees
idealism in science
what a fucked up
paycheck.
Lest I forget him,
how he knew where to find me
when I hid
and took me to every quiet
nook
to ravish me
and wake up parts of me
my young heart
still searches for.
Sitting in a waiting room
is not
my favorite place
but we must
do it
the only thing left to do
is remember
think some more
remember some more.

Say goodnight, good morning
find patience and vending machines
coffee moka awful blends
sour cream and onion chips
suddenly there are no candy bars
going crazy looking for snickers
remember the way
back form the cafeteria
memorize letters
get lost in basements
ask at least two strangers
for directions
and count my change.
Say good night again.
And start over.

Ticket Train

Look up and watch the fall sky.
I keep on waiting
for the perfect day
to burn the notes
but they remain intact
an abstract Pollock painting
locked up
in some burgundy chest
bought at Winners.
No one holds the lock and key
as tightly as you do.
Even if you knew me then
against the high school wall
or now
as I wait in the sky
or in the future
writing you in my life
none of it would matter
except half-hour dates
and minutes to destiny
as love affairs
come and go
like snowstorms
leaving me under
to feel the freezing water
waiting to melt
at his warming touch
and thaw out
under his skin.

Murders in Montreal
rapists in hiding
driving on Sherbrooke Street
looking for tattoo parlours
to imprint your soul
upon my skin
as if it could even
be done.
None of it is real.
What a lively imagination
you have
just listen and maybe
you will hear the birds too
in -20 degrees
Tiffany did, she told
me so this morning.
I lit a candle for her
for her cat-scan
for her life.
I keep on praying for others
who will ever pray for me?
I know the dead do.
The only ones I can rely on.

Floating Above my Deadline

If you want fire
light up a smoke,
it's been too long
since I inhaled
your toxic words.
I am lounging
around, letting the cold air
fill my lungs.
Dragged from one city
to another in a state
of loss. Loss of the
astute ways you nudge
my knees apart
from the outskirts
of your town. Walls restrict
and leave me to build
fondness
admiration
of your fossilized words
that can bury me
under the frozen rivers
of this province.
I dreamed that you loved me
as you were meant to,
that you spoke to me,
as you would like to,
clearly
I saw your lips move
first in front of mine
soon after they traveled
along my frontiers.

It seems uncivilized to chase
a fox
yet honeyed words
will make most women
contradict and fool
even themselves.
She should stop.
She should go.
She should stop and go.
I teach my son how to drive
how to treat a woman
how to love
how to surpass men
and reach out and touch a soul.
He can do it. I have faith.
I cross my fingers as I wait
to see if my breasts
will continue to bring me
joy or pain.
I float above all my deadlines
punching numbers
and faces of years gone by.
I suppose it is best to dig up
the skeletons
tell you
how they sleep.
Best to add mortar
to my brick walls
peek through a crack
as I fade
paint

a new landscape
from my third eye.
Old past loves
never wave good-bye.
His last true words
carved into my heart
like the couples' initials
forever on Mont-Royal.
Ink my name
on your skin
you talk about it so often
just do it
so you can be
reminded of how
I broke your heart.
Share a drink with me
one more time
give me everything in one hour
to last
years
meet me at the corner of Rue d'Amour
and Rue Je t'adore.
It exists
somewhere
we have never been before.

My New York Way

Everything sounds divine
with a hint of you and some red wine
had to Google a few places
to get to the lines on your face
the Virgo in me is awake
can't sleep in a cold lake
next time around in another lifetime
you'll meet me at the drop of a dime
at Strand in the poetry section
drinking doubles at the W Hotel
a sexual addiction
fuck the shows and the shops
water and cheesecake drops
don't need WiFi
for my way into the deep entry of my silent sigh
for the true artiste in *moi*
wants a glimpse of hotel bars
not merely sheets
drinks and sliding beats
we won't come up for air
you better just sit there and stare
at my hokey pokey naked dance
you're sure to be in a sick trance
I think there is more at the museum
but I lost my way at the lobby
lost my wallet and my mind
still I never lose sight of your kind
and rough verse
your silent twisted curse

it's a gift I know
sometimes I'd rather not put on this show
but the need overrides the logic
and the rush of words so tragic
hitting the ground
in a lovers' exhaustion
another round
of love with no caution.
Changing checking time
to another poetic rhyme
so we could capture the sunset
and let go of the butterfly net.

Twelve Steps to Writing

1.
Waiting
for handwritten notes
to be gently placed
into the palm
of my tiny hand.

2.
Waiting
for your poems
like a drug addict
in the depths
of the need.

3.
Waiting
for your inspiration
to take full control
of my thoughts
and leave behind
my car
in an abandoned parking lot
to find your crumbs.

4.
Waiting
for nothing to happen
but Silence
as my mind
reads yours
through distance and time
along
gravelled 1920's train tracks.

5.
Waiting
to be divided
by a doorway
stepped on clothes
as you fling
my body across
your shoulder
and spank my naked ass.

6.
Waiting
for the breakdown
to pass
but you must know
how I can breathe
freely
underwater
like a true mermaid.

7.
Waiting
to create
sensual art
with your fingers
as brushstrokes
and my body
your blank canvas.

8.
Waiting
to be undressed
slowly
and
thoughtfully
by your picture
smooth hands
clasping the wheel.

9.
Waiting
on years
and decades
for something
so romantic
candles and ghosts
will feel.

10.
Waiting
for old poetry lines
and lovers
to burn
as others can't
compare
to the desire
in our lair.

11.
Waiting
for the cold snap
to pass
and the heat
from within
to bring you closer
to my wanting love.

12.
Waiting
is my secret
in peace
as a comfort
to my thousand year old soul
that knows yours so well.

Magic Hands

You play the songs
say the write words
get me inside out
understand my coffee stops
late night alcoholic binges
cigarette traps
eternal fights
then you throw me on the bed
and all is forgotten.
You know all the thoughts
before I speak
yet still there is always more
to want and need
as one kiss remains
surmountable
climbing up that hill
every day
to get to this
point
of magical hands
all over the flesh.
I never listen.
I chase my own demons
and entrap them
with my wit
as even *they*
confuse my day and night
my night with flight
my pain with joy

as words build invisible
love affairs
so do love affairs
build sweet heartache
to continue the words
that save us.

Fate

you said to leave it to fate
don't make a date
the time "who cares"
the meeting
well, who dares.
Ain't it funny how
time knocks us down now
how New York
was a daunting force
to carry me like a running horse
to your steps
in the cab in Brooklyn
we giggled and cried and this losing win
you get in my head
for a second
you get in my bed
and I would reckon
God would be hated
we would be jaded.
Even Aphrodite agrees
and Apollo he decrees
that lovers like us
make great statues
cupid & psyche
writing the blues.
I did dance at The W
with a good-looking crew
smoking on the street
I thought I saw you

but my heart didn't skip a beat
in Times Square
and fuck I thought
"Life is not fair."
And another week rolls by
and more tears I will surely cry
for you know you'll always be the one
I don't play dumb.
Third time is never a charm
it's bullshit, causing more harm
better to go see Andy Warhol alone
sit on the steps you call home
and feel your presence
in your absence.

Needs

Words need an exit
for writers.
Readers need
an entrance.
Some poems are meant
to be read aloud
lying naked in bed
drinking up each other's
words.
Inhaling and exhaling words
skipping meals
poets are meant to look
into each other's eyes
with no sunglasses
no lies.
Eliminate your disguise
and melt with me
onto the sheets
disappear on a break
run from the calls.
Sleeping in another galaxy.
Montreal is perfect
for summer acts
of love
and Art
Poetry
Music
Now I've emptied out my mind
replaced it with your poses.

You could have been
a model
but really
I could not care less
if your eyes were purple
For it is your one thousand year
old soul that speaks
to me
and recognizes our memories.
It could not have been
one mere lifetime
But many.
So many I refuse to breathe.
Disappearing behind
my typewriter
to recall
and write my stories.

Poetry Dance

You ask me to do the poetry dance
as my hands are tied but never free
diving into a dangerous chance
to unwind the words of the sea
make them twirl
bend to our whim
let the pain unfurl
for I am always aching for him
that illusion of hope
living on the edge of Broadway
refusing to hand over that rope
mixing up my night with my day
my poems with reality.
Let us dance and swallow our moving words
like we did on scraped knees way back when
embrace the sky, fly like birds
for we are far to gaze into each others' eyes
too close to sleep a whole night through
toss and turn me with burning lies.
I am not like them. I do not scrub
bathtubs until I am heart broken.
I do eat men while I walk to the cafe.
I do not see dust
I see poetry.
I like the rhymes
distracted by the underlying chimes.
I am in love with the man
who stole my heart
yet the dance in my soul
stops moving its feet.

I read all the dead poets
it is the only way I can have my coffee
they are my cream and sugar
the poets that live
try
but those folded (yellowed) pages
in my Norton Anthology of Modern Poetry
are my only salvation
from men such as you
who can eat me alive.
You can caress my hair
and my soul at the same time.
I do not make grocery lists
search for discounts
make the bed
I am not the best wife
for you will find me under the fan smoking
with my notebook
on the kitchen table
writing
and the meal long forgotten.
I like how he snores, though
wakes me up and begins my writing
finding comfort in the sounds around me
while I pour out my ink once more.
The only way to continue breathing
is to dance
let the words tickle my sex
encompass my fear
rip open my guts

but you should stand back
because I am always at the edge of seventeen
(as Stevie Nicks sings)
and poets like you
inhale my words
regurgitate them
while poets like me
drown at Cosco.

Chasing the Honey Moon

He once brought me so high
I swear I could have touched the sky
then he murdered me piece by piece
left my heart for last
I actually did lay on the floor
my sex in the grips of his hand
moaning his name
crying as he fled out the door
proclaiming how he would always love me
but I leave him no other choice
I can't use only lust on him
he wants me to give him
that part I hold on to
so desperately.
Under the honey moon
I take a drive with the kids
yelling to find it, where is it,
but my smart son says it's cloudy
can't see it, I guess you'll have to
wait another hundred years
and I want to stop the tears
but I can't
stupid fucking moon I say
and they laugh and know
to watch me carefully
because I will get lost
on the same road
thinking of you.
They know they shouldn't ask
why I want to find it so badly

I wish I had the answer as well
but it leaves me empty inside
sticking my head out the window
I only see grey
and taste the acid rain on my lips
blending perfectly with my tears.
Play me a song from your phone
I tell my son
but he's into Rush this week
no, go back
and he is the only one
who knows the playlist of my heart
let's start with Dreams
he tells me.
Now the dark grey skies mean no harm
It's in my head I tell myself
as Van Halen plays
but
Plath's words hit me right then and there
and I repeat them
There's no way out of the mind.

Only One

I like when I am the only one
doing my cross and kissing your image
only dead souls
under my feet
and I can't speak to you
I feel blocked
no birds flying
I wait for a sign
but someone blasts music
from behind the Marble Jesus
and I keep it buried
where you are
wanting to join you.
But I check the candle
read the sentiment
examine the Greek letters
the year you were born and died
remember my book
cry as usual
squat and stare at your eyes
kiss the stone
and go to the grocery store.

Anniversary

Burgundy velvet interior
Godfather scenes
we held smooth hands
bonded with devoted plans
some underground
visible, and invisible.
We giggled, yes, you held my heart
with your devious blue eyes
Coffee cup on Anne
bite marks on my neck
well hidden
dancing to the sounds
no one else could hear
first there was the downpour
then all became clear
judging my love with the weather
looking for signs in a dead feather
then we pressed our fresh faces
in the back of the limousine
for a snapshot
in black and white film.
Red roses, white flowers in my dark hair
Pablo Neruda quotes
hand painted angels with hand written tiny
notes.
The artist in me made you swell
you made that? Hand painted each note? You chose
red?
Yet, my love, by the time you said

I love your ways
I blocked my ears
and ran for a while.
The moment came and went
lightning and thunder
entered me
I care too much about timing
reading to you in bed
Tropic of Cancer
and then you loved him too
you said don't ever stop
and Now I do.
What are you doing? I don't even reply.
My pen is on fire
burning ashes
on the lines
no one can reach me
in that place where I belong
no one can stop me at Second Cup
and ask me what went wrong.
This day is sealed within us
we flew to London, Greece
and slept where Gods slept
as your Spartan shield
protected me
as it did from the start
when you tiptoed into my broken heart.

Marie

I wear a fishu
regard words with judgement
eat fresh croissants
close to Palais-Royal
and watch you arrive
with hope and ideals
about the future of France
amongst my wax sculptures
poking their head at you
and embarking on the journey
that is destined for free thinkers
such as us.
I will marry you one day
handsome genius
of air balloons
but first my audience
awaits.
The struggle continues
on blvd du Temple
but you support
the artistry
the passion
you can only wait
for so long
to make me your woman.
I have my own path.
When you hold me
I forget how hard my hands work
or the royalty

there is only you and me
as it should be
but your art comes first, you plead
for all my denial
you know me well
and next year
perhaps you will not know me
at all.

For you, The Reader

Not sure about the quota
the stats
for the day
but I cannot switch it off.
My Reader says,
I read you breathlessly
eager to ingest
every word
like hard liquor
burning my insides.
(And here I thought
I was nothing special
full of self-doubt
and betrayal).
Do I excite you? In what way?
To hold me close
to smell my skin
to part my legs
and feel me from within?
I know about the phases.
I read Neruda's sonnets
the morning, the afternoon, the evening
and I feel his currents
sweep me into his waves
that crash against my body.
I'm truly a romantic fool
yet so alive
with wonder
like a little girl
lost in a shopping mall.

When I see the wicked words
I want to bathe naked in them.
Can you imagine such a scene?
Shredded paper in the floating water.
I am sure you would comply
if I ask such strange requests.
You open up my soul
these words
come out like waterfall
with no self-control
no edits.
I stop washing dishes
forget to eat
all to get this cough of words
stuck in my throat
to you,
whether you read me or not
others need it too.
Now I get stopped in the street
my identity no longer hushed
I love your poems
I read them every day
Please keep them coming
so this one is for you, my Reader
the ones that connect
the dotted lines
into their very own
heartbeat.

Crystal Soul

It is not fair when you say
you would love me forever
and then never show up to prove it
words are just pebbles
and love is just the ocean
but actions and gestures
are the steps
to make my heart shake
my soul has already
been spoken for
do not ask to conquer it
for it is futile
worthless, unattainable
it has been claimed before
I was born
before you were born
my soul has travelled
endless waters
to come to me
I am sure others tried to claim it
for it is truly
a crystal soul
you can see all the shimmering light
if you step close to me
you have to almost
walk through me
to appreciate the glitter
and the reflections
but so far

no one has even attempted
to open me up
once-almost happened
twice-I ran home
and now
I wait
for my other light
to complete me.

Broken Glass

It smashes
into smithereens
can get caught in your knee
when you save a life
it carries my wine
and brings me moments of pleasure
until I drop it
and sweep up the pieces.
I walked right into its darkness
two o'clock in the afternoon
right after I downloaded Blondie
how ironic, I thought
while carrying a blue body out of debris
actually I was on adreniline
and survival and all the glass
could not touch me
make me bleed, yes
shock me, yes.
I was seven the first time it happened
my foot in a bowl full of grass
that my grandma cut up and boiled.
My head hit the dash but I survived
we were seven in a car
and back in 1975 everything seemed legal.
In 2013, my life flashed before my eyes
but I didn't die.

I had to save a few lives first
before mine fell apart.
Broken glass can do that to you
break your heart in pieces
you keep on collecting
years and decades later.
No matter how many poems
I write
it cannot be forgotten
I ignore it and pretend it never
happened. I disassociate
I drink. And then it comes back
and cuts me up
inside with its sharp double edges.
Glass can damage wood, tile, ceramic
entrances, doors, windows,
hearts and souls. And sometimes
it kills, but not me.
I survived it.
I survived my own flood
and broken glass.
I wrote it in a poem
and watched it die.

I will always be a mystery even to myself.

Acknowledgements

I thank you the reader first and foremost. I thank you for reading my poetry and acknowledging my voice. It took years to type it all out and present it, but I was never ready before to share my work. Remember to love the poem and not the poet.

There are moments of truth we have to live and others we are only able to write about. The gift of writing could be a curse as well. While others sleep and go about their daily rituals, I am observing how the sky matches his eyes. Words pass through me and I try to grasp them all. I tried my best to present to you a poetry book that has captured all my voices. I hope you enjoyed it and I really hope you pass around my book so others can read it too. I hope this book in your hands is shared with loved ones and it can touch as many souls as possible. Even if it has touched one soul, that is enough for me.

Thank you to my husband who loves all of me and accepts my craziness.

If writing hurts, you're doing it right.

My website and blog:
www.christinastrigas.com
Twitter: @christinastriga
Facebook: Christina Strigas Author
Instagram: c.strigas_sexyasspoet
email: christinastrigasauthor@gmail.com

About the Author

Christina Strigas writes poetry and novels. This is her third poetry book. She lives in Montreal with her husband and two children. You can check out her books on Amazon or any on-line bookstore. Her poetry books are only in print format.

CPSIA information can be obtained
at www.ICGtesting.com
Printed in the USA
LVHW08s1350100918
589685LV00021B/1052/P